WCW

Battle Royal!	5
WCW Fact File: RAVISHING RICK RUDE	27
WCW Fact File: STING	28
WCW Fact File: Z-MAN	29
Sting's Metal Mayhem!	30
WCW Fact File: EL GIGANTE	35
WCW Superstar Super Moves	36
WCW Fact File: JOHNNY B. BADD	39
WCW Fact File: P.N. NEWS	40
Heel!	41

WCW WORLD CHAMPIONSHIP WRESTLING ANNUAL 1993 is published by MARVEL COMICS LTD., 13/15 Arundel Street, London WC2R 3DX. WCW WORLD CHAMPIONSHIP WRESTLING, including all prominent characters featured in this annual and the distinctive likenesses thereof, are trademarks of WORLD CHAMPIONSHIP WRESTLING, INC. All WCW WORLD CHAMPIONSHIP WRESTLING material copyright ©1992 WORLD CHAMPIONSHIP WRESTLING, INC. All rights reserved. Licensed by Turner Home Entertainment, Inc. All other material copyright ©1992 Marvel Comics Ltd. All rights reserved. No similarity between any of the names, characters, persons, and/or institutions in this magazine with those of any living or dead person or institution is intended, and any such similarity which may exist is purely coincidental. Printed in Italy.

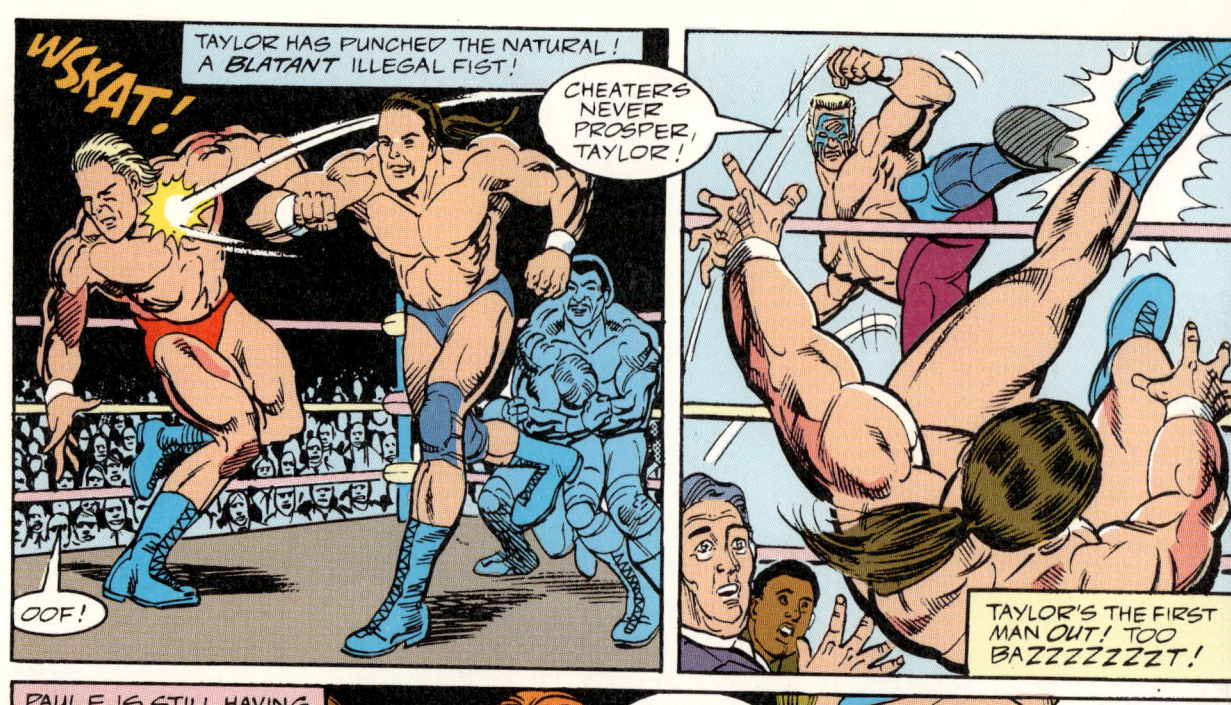

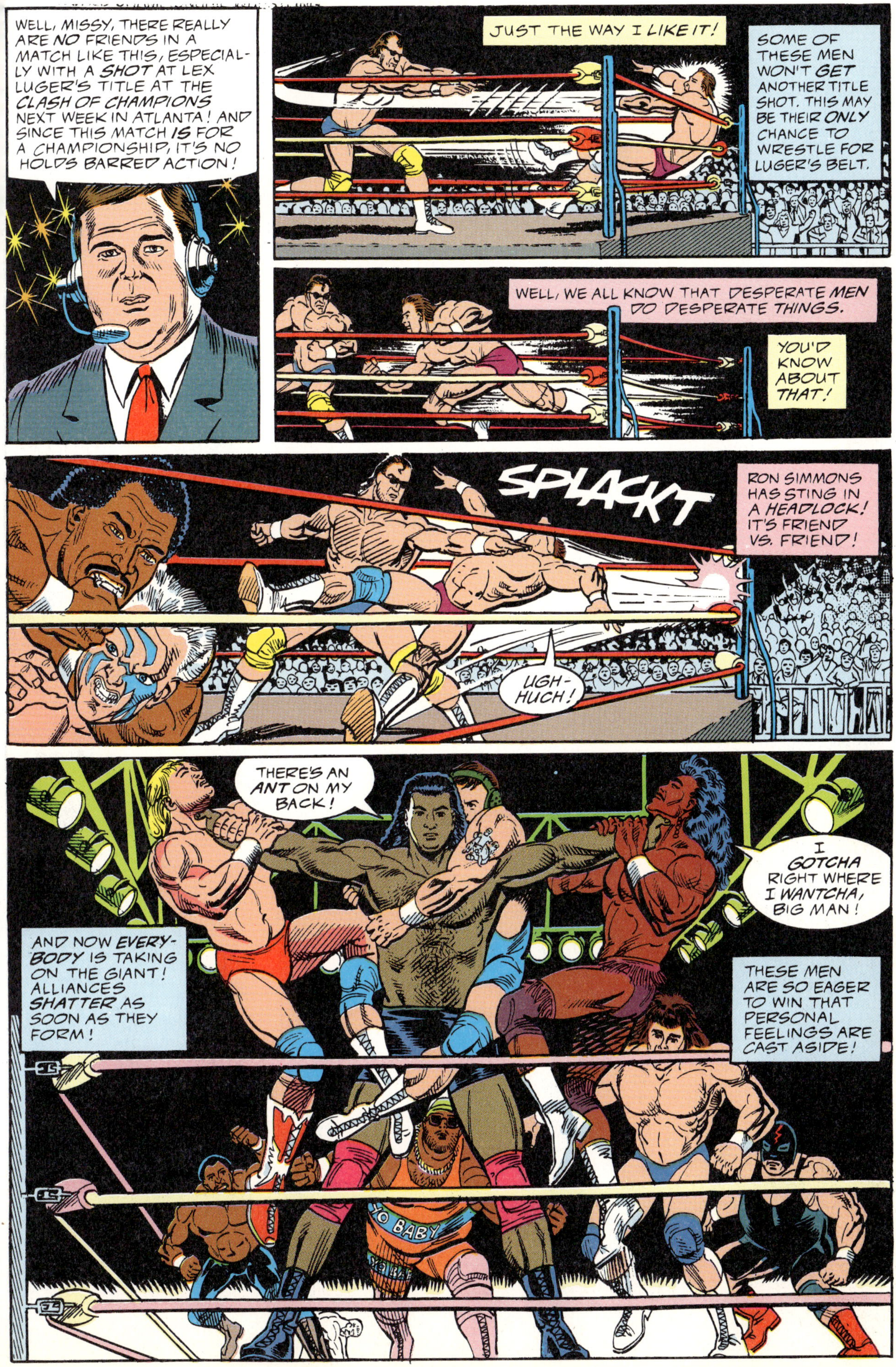

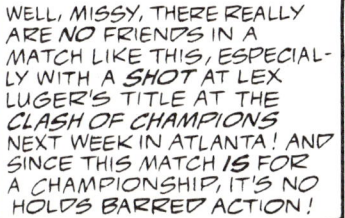

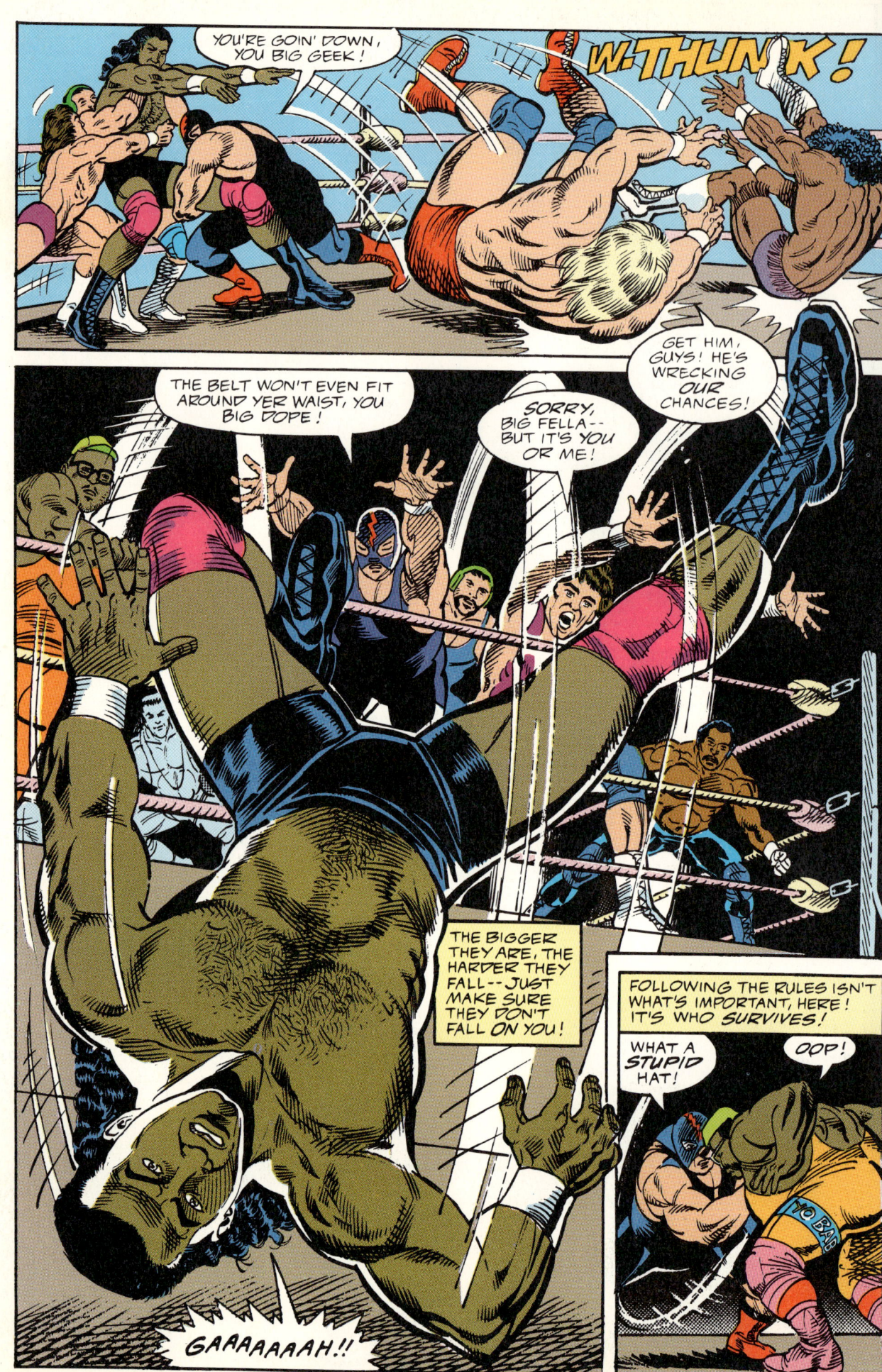

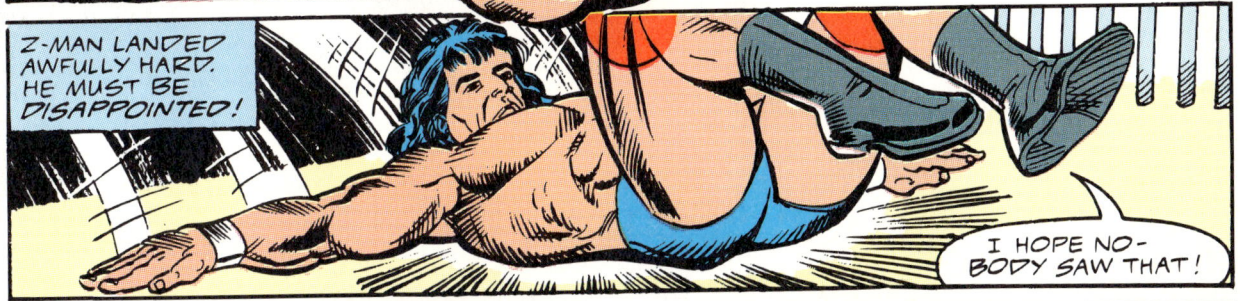

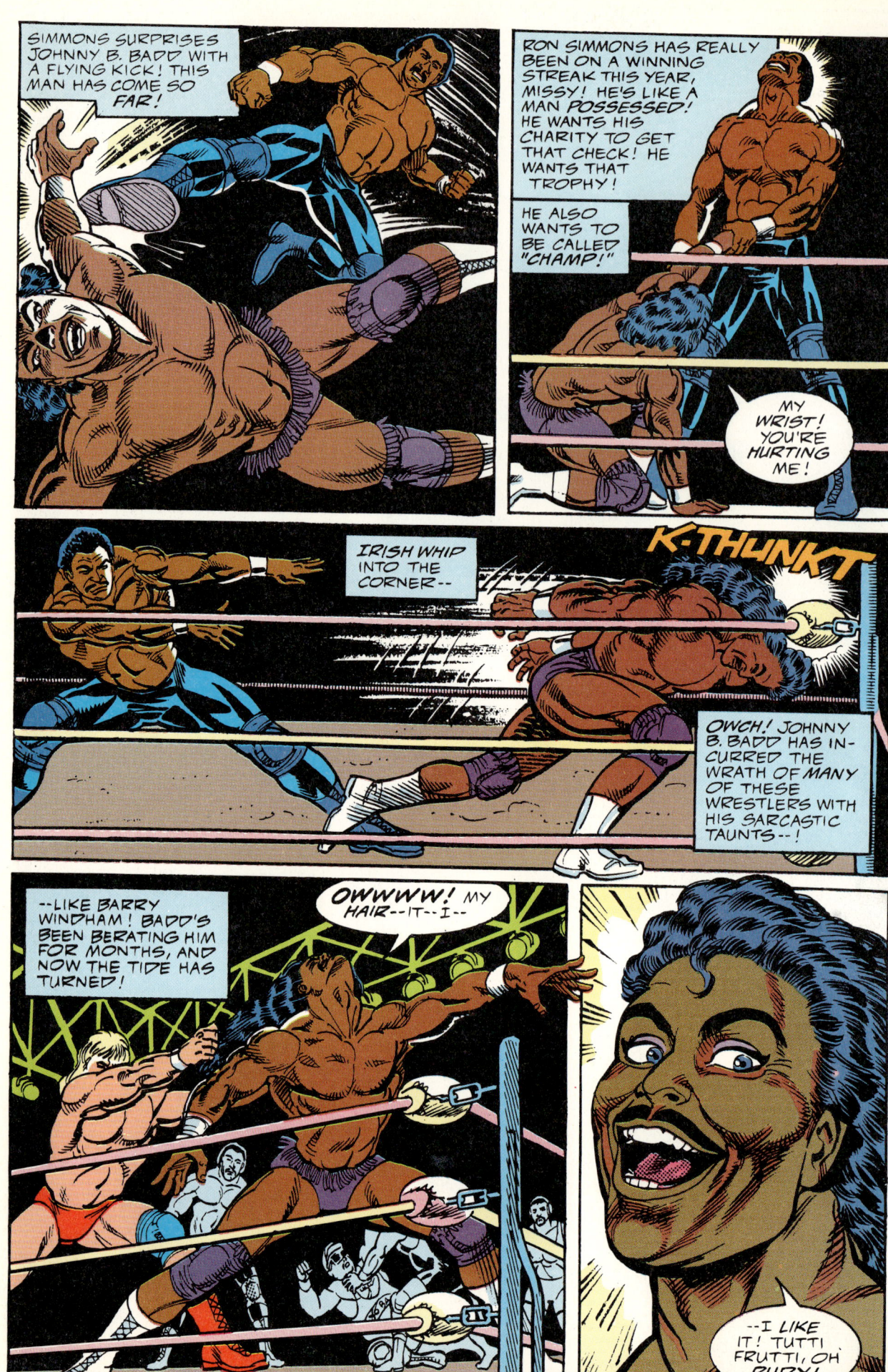

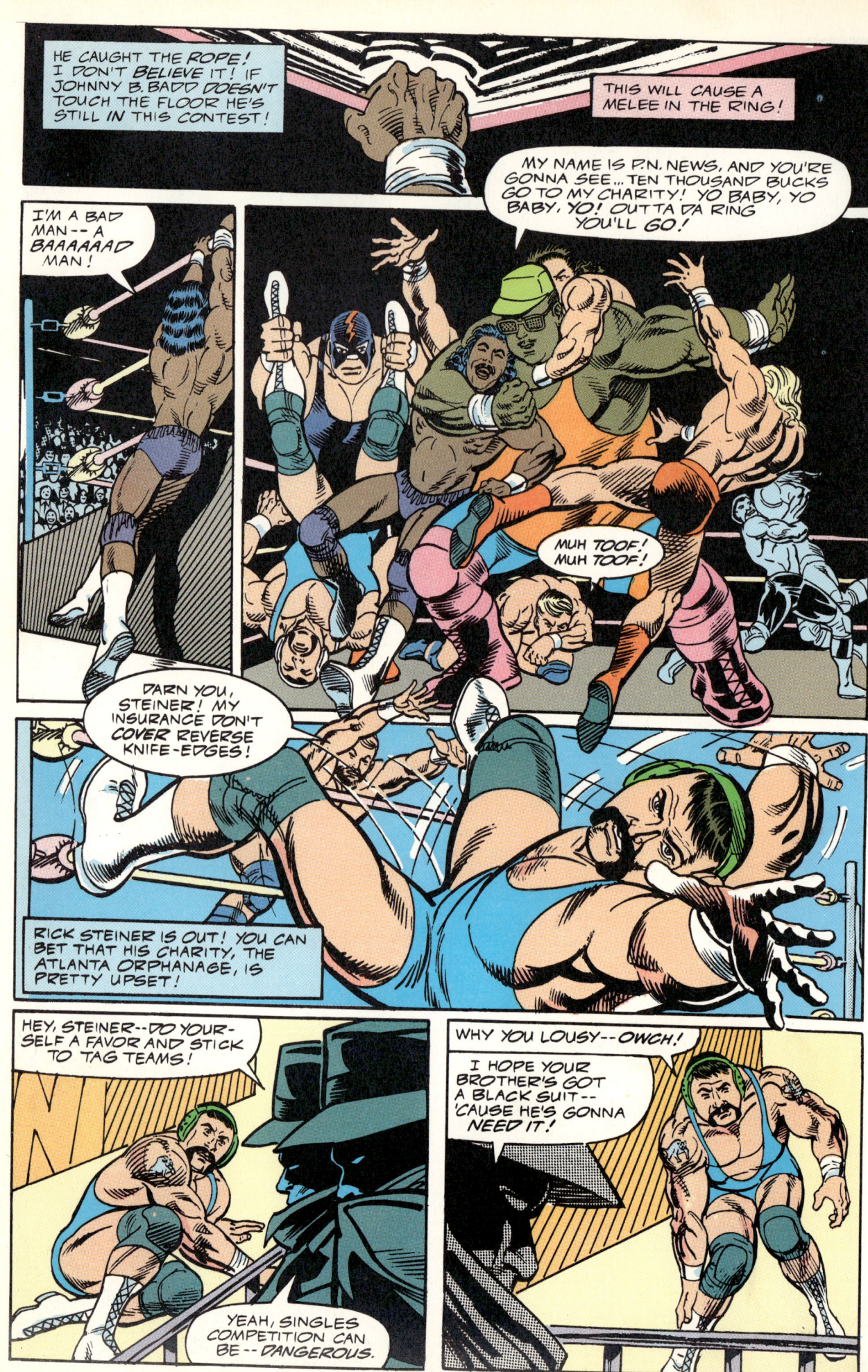

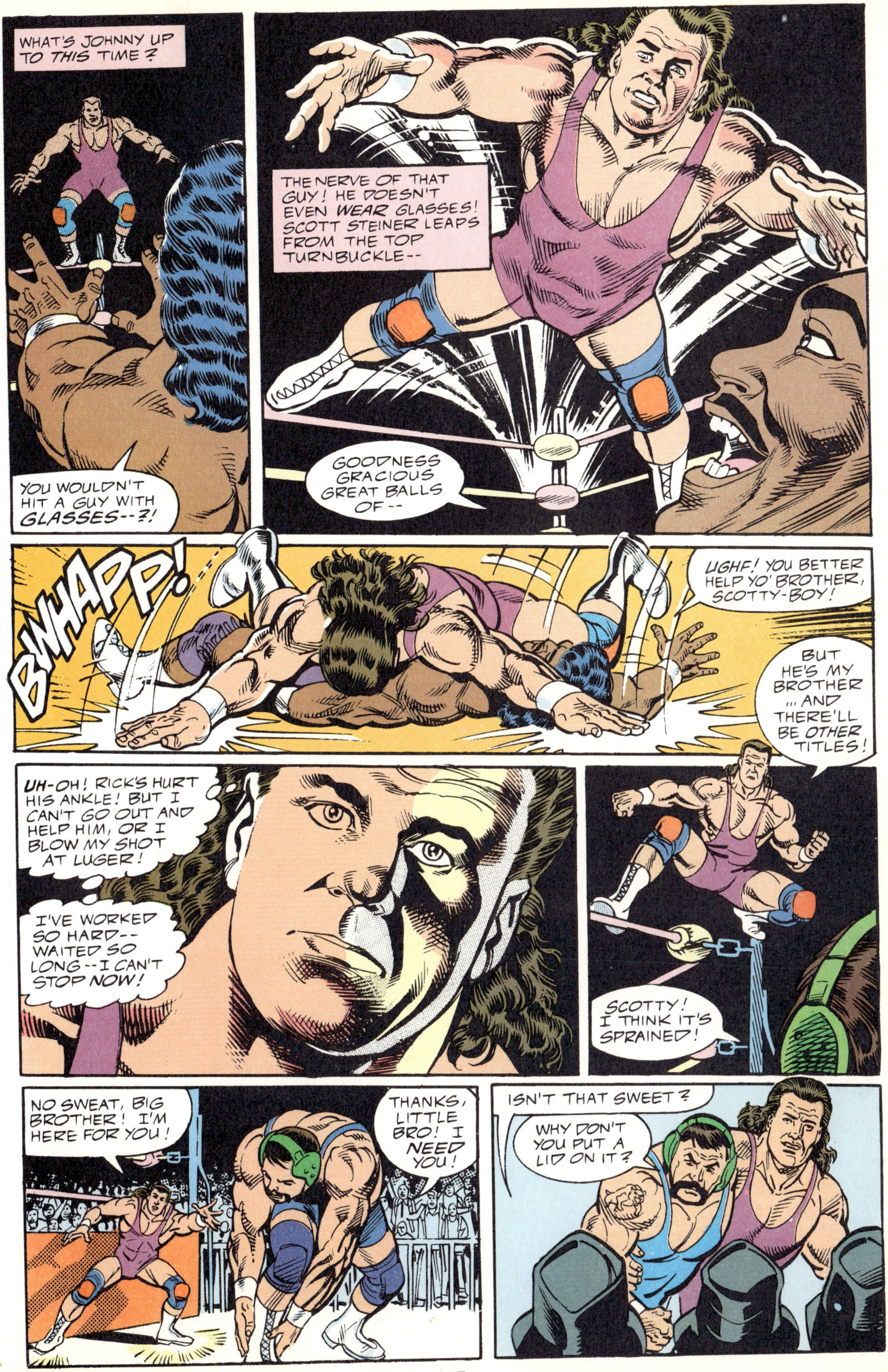

WHAT'S JOHNNY UP TO *THIS* TIME?

THE NERVE OF THAT GUY! HE DOESN'T EVEN *WEAR* GLASSES! SCOTT STEINER LEAPS FROM THE TOP TURNBUCKLE--

YOU WOULDN'T HIT A GUY WITH *GLASSES*--?!

GOODNESS GRACIOUS GREAT BALLS OF--

BWHAPP!

UGHF! YOU BETTER HELP YO' BROTHER, SCOTTY-BOY!

BUT HE'S MY BROTHER... AND THERE'LL BE OTHER TITLES!

UH-OH! RICK'S HURT HIS ANKLE! BUT I CAN'T GO OUT AND HELP HIM, OR I BLOW MY SHOT AT LUGER!

I'VE WORKED SO HARD-- WAITED SO LONG-- I CAN'T STOP NOW!

SCOTTY! I THINK IT'S SPRAINED!

NO SWEAT, BIG BROTHER! I'M HERE FOR YOU!

THANKS, LITTLE BRO! I NEED YOU!

ISN'T THAT SWEET? WHY DON'T YOU PUT A LID ON IT?

15

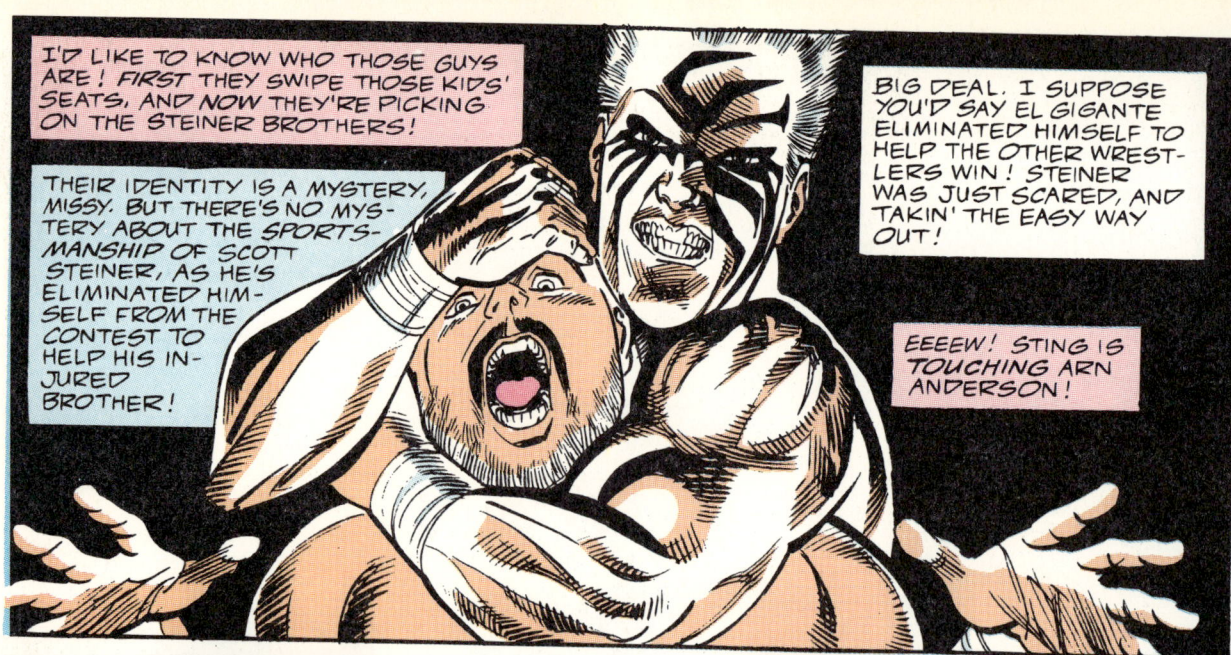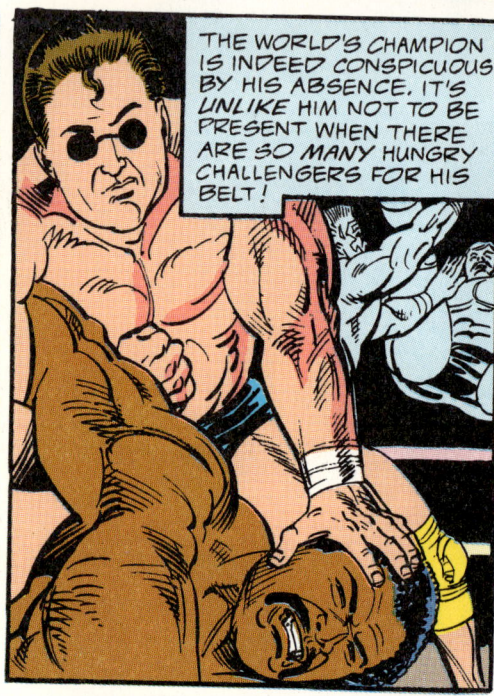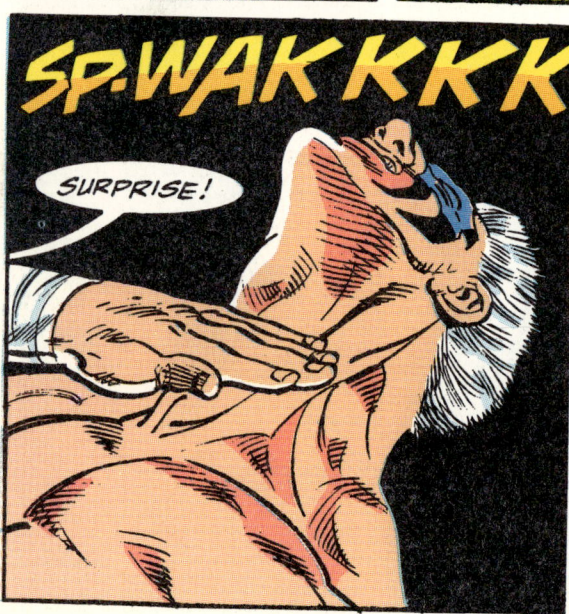

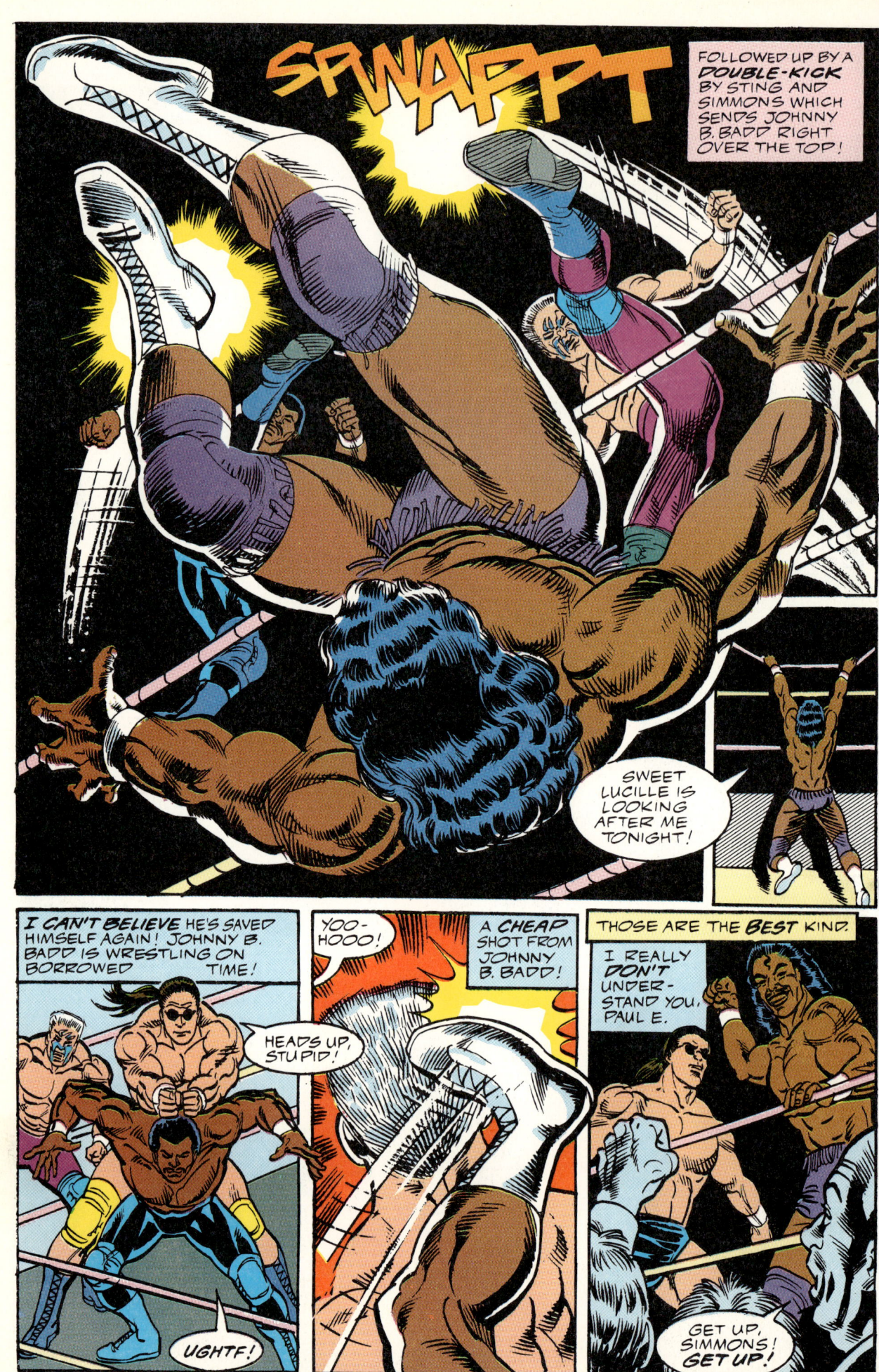

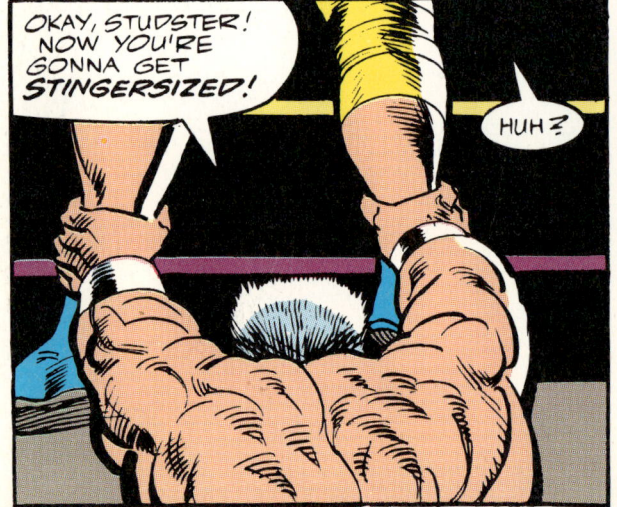

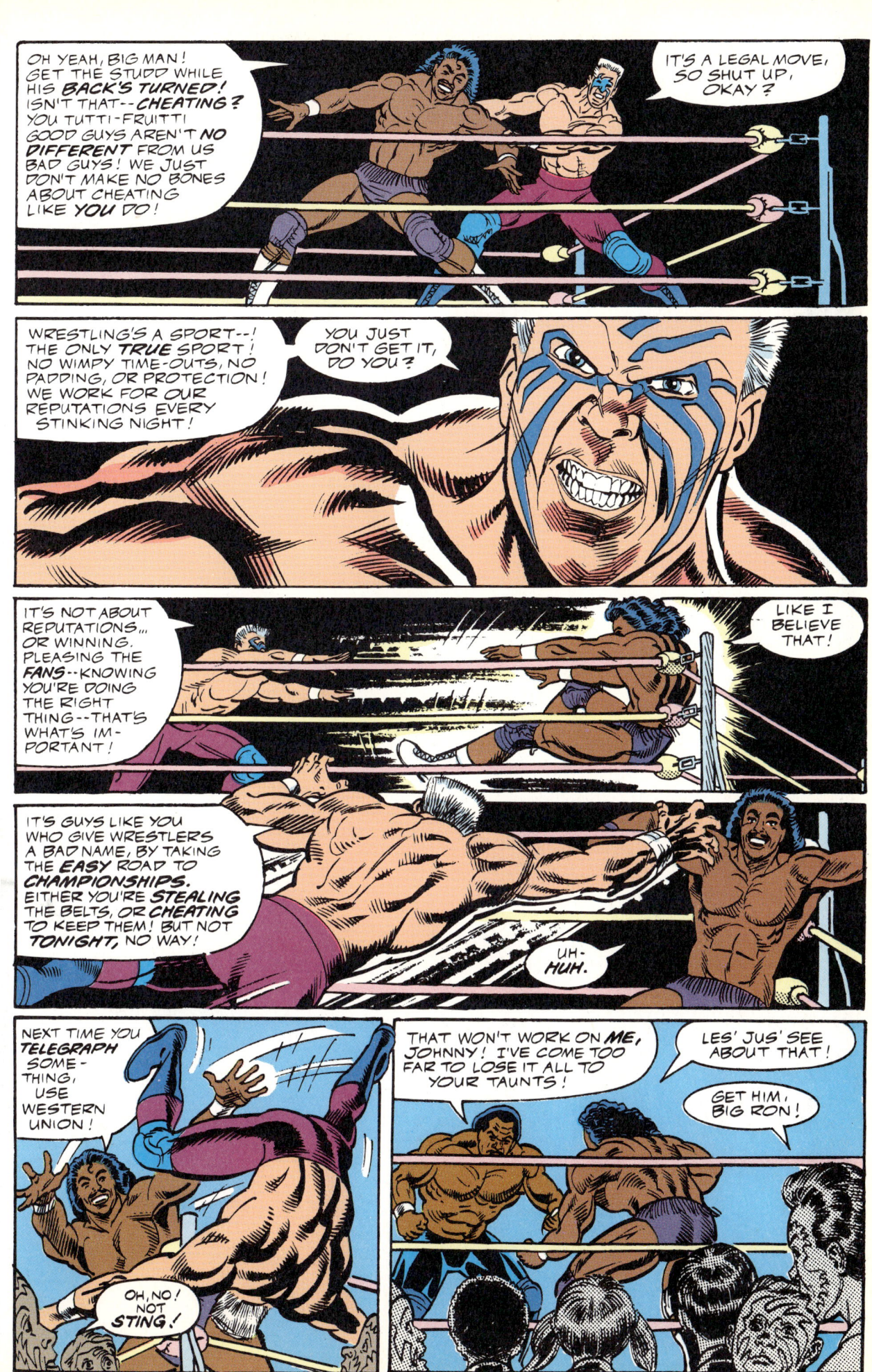

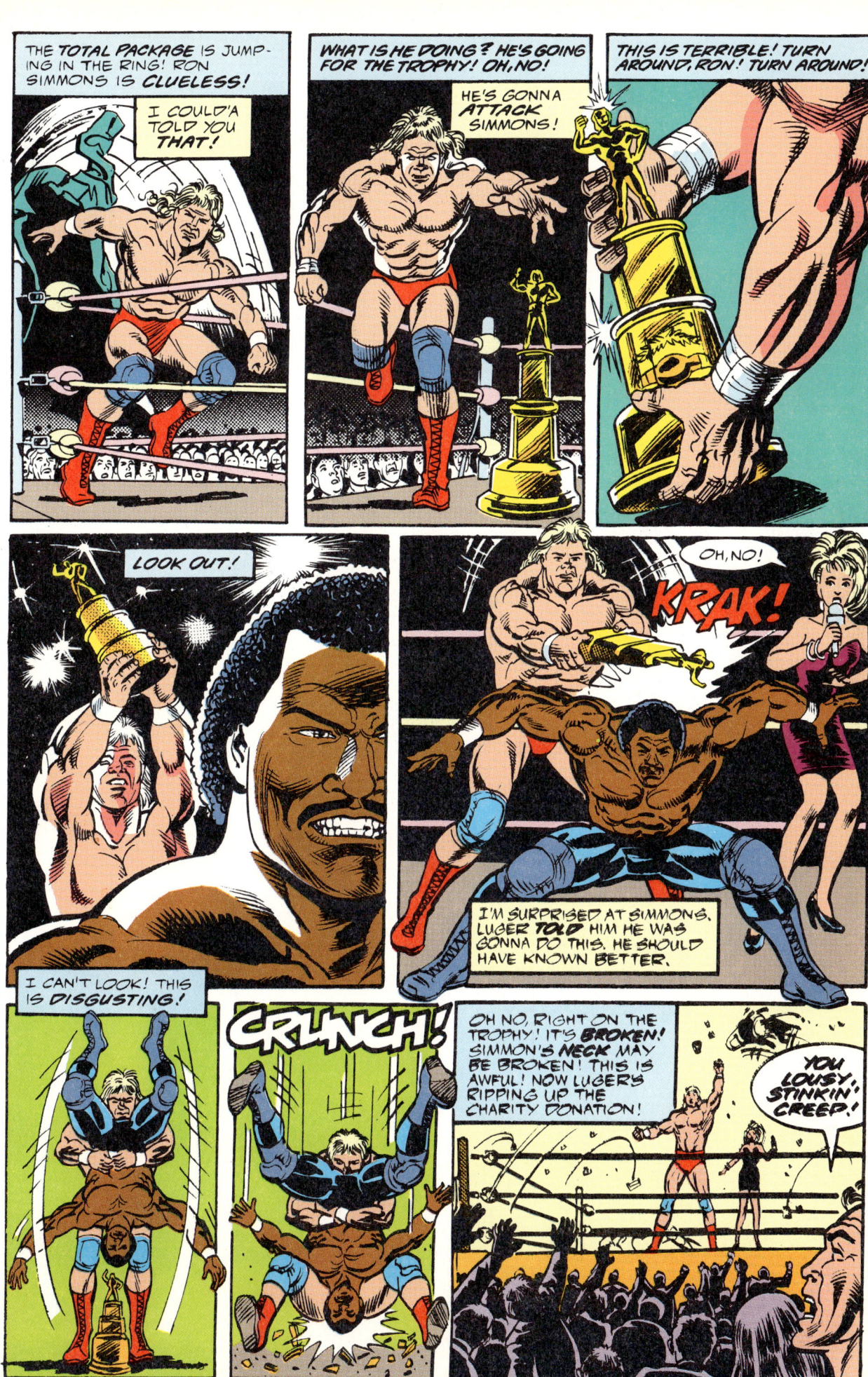

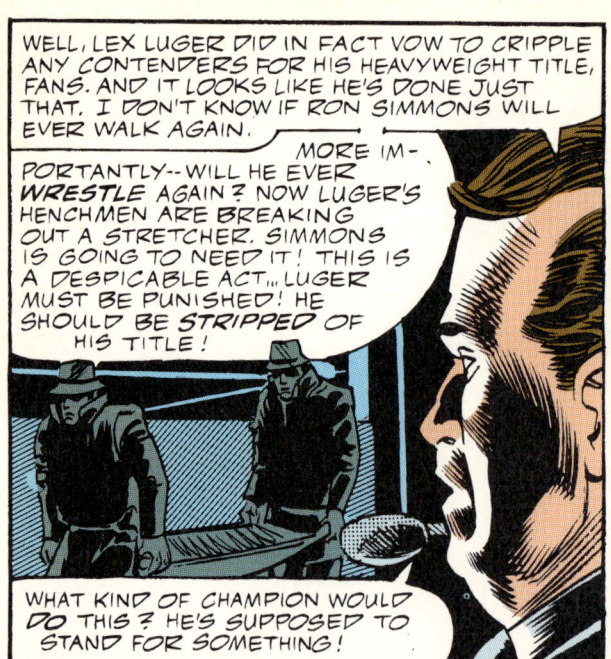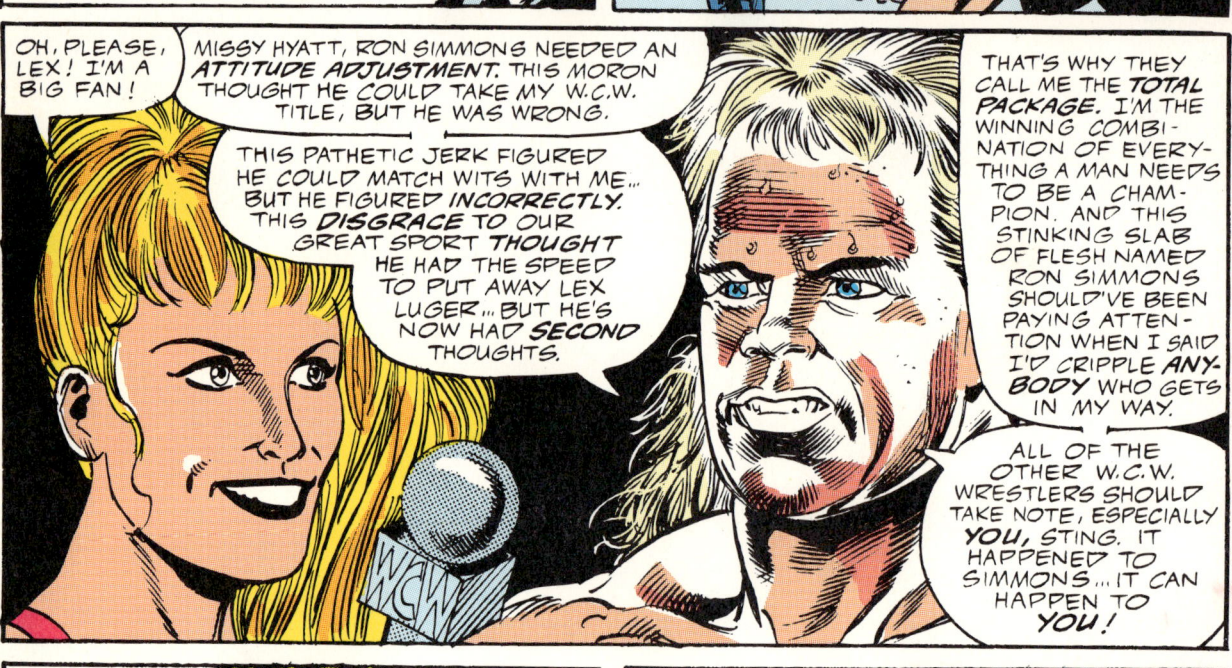

WCW

'RAVISHING' RICK RUDE

From his entrance into the ring with his snake-like movement and chant "Turn down the music, I have something to say!", everything about Rick Rude exudes arrogance. Since he first entered the world of WCW, he has had only one goal - to single-handedly take over WCW and become the next world heavyweight champion. With his awesome wrestling manoeuvres and the devastating "Rude Awakening" that bring his opponents to their knees begging for mercy, this man is simply ravishing.

Height: 6'5"
Weight: 252lb

Hometown: Robinsdale, Minnesota.
Favourite Hold: Rude Awakening.
Favourite Pastimes: Fast cars, fast women and fast sports.
Motto: "Anybody that knows Ravishing Rick Rude knows that all I care about is myself, my women and my money!"

WCW

STING

Coming into professional wrestling with a vengeance, **Sting** has had an unparalleled impact on the wrestling world. The Venice Beach native's weightlifting programme spurred his interest in professional wrestling and prepared him for the nightly rigours of the sport. A naturally talented athlete, Sting excelled in basketball, football and track in High School and continues to perfect his surfing abilities. Sting possesses a potent grip when he wrestles, creating a fearful look in the eyes of his opponents. With his youth and powerful, deadly holds, The Stinger currently holds the World Heavyweight title.

Height: 6'3"
Weight: 262 lbs

Hometown: Venice Beach, California
Favourite Holds: Scorpion Deathlock, Stinger Splash
Toughest Opponent: Ravishing Rick Rude
Greatest Achievement: Winning the World Heavyweight Championship
Motto: "We're having fun now!"

WCW

Z- MAN

Sporting one of the best physiques in professional wrestling today, "Z-Man", Tom Zenk has made his mark in World Championship Wrestling. A former Mr Minnesota, "Z-Man" uses his tremendous strength and agility to unleash devastating dropkicks and a sleeper hold that few opponents can escape.

Height: 6'2"
Weight: 250 lbs

Hometown: Minnetonka, Minnesota
Favourite Holds: Drop Kick, Sleeper
Toughest Opponents: Unknown
Greatest Achievement: Winning the U.S. Tag-Team belt
Motto: "Stay single"

Sting paced the wrestling ring with all the power and grace of a caged tiger. His magnificently muscled body rippled with strength, ready to explode into action. Tonight Sting would compete in an unique wrestling match, because tonight Sting had no idea **who** his opponent would be!

The strange affair had begun when Paul E. Dangerously, manager of the Dangerous Alliance, had challenged Sting, as on of **WCW**'s top ranking wrestlers, to a match. However, the identity of the Dangerous Alliance's wrestler had not been revealed. No wrestler wanted to enter the square ring unprepared for their opponent, but Sting had accepted the challenge regardless, and a date had been set for the tour.

Thousands of eager fans had flocked to the arena for the mystery match, and the wrestling world was buzzing with anticipation. Who would the unknown wrestler be? Paul E. Dangerously had kept security tight on his latest scheme to dominate WCW. Whatever he was planning, it would be computer-tested for its chances of success, for his use of state-of-the-art computer technology was well-known within the WCW Federation.

Sting continued his warm-up exercises in the ring, his painted face a grim mask of determination. Suddenly, the house lights dimmed and a hush fell upon the crowd as a wave of anticipation spread throughout the packed arena. A lone spotlight fell upon the curtain entrance through which Sting's opponent would enter. The curtains drew back. There, bathed in the spotlight, was Paul E. Dangerously, a chubby, balding man dressed in a smart business suit, and as always carrying his portable telephone in his hand. Paul E. Dangerously strode forward, a smug look on his face as he walked towards the ring.

Members of the audience near to the entrance leaned over the crowd

barriers, trying to see who the mystery opponent would be. Several steps behind Paul E. Dangerously came Sting's adversary.

The crowd couldn't believe their eyes. Sting couldn't believe his eyes. No matter how hard he had trained, there was no way he could have prepared himself for such opposition. Now Sting knew why Paul E. Dangerously was smirking as he approached the ring; his mystery wrestler was...**a robot!**

As the mechanical wrestler glided effortlessly toward the ring its steel limbs glistened in the light. Its expressionless face turned towards Sting without a trace of mercy or emotion in its burning red eyes.

Paul E. Dangerously looked up at Sting and taunted the blond giant.

"What's the matter, Sting? Afraid of my wrestler?" he sneered.

"You can't enter a robot into a wrestling match," he protested. "It's against WCW rules".

"This robot has been programmed with *every* wrestling move in the rule book," snapped Paul E. Dangerously.

" I think you're afraid to face it because it's **faster** and **stronger** than you."

Sting looked down at the massive robot waiting motionless at the ringside. He could see his own reflection in its shiny, steel face covering. Then Sting looked out at the stunned crowd. He knew that if he backed out of the match now, he would disappoint them. Many of the young fans, **the Stingers**, looked up to him. He couldn't let them down. He *wouldn't* let them down.

"Get in here!" Sting shouted to the robot. "**Let's wrestle!**"

Instantly the robot leaped into the ring, its servo motors buzzing into deadly life. This robot was as fast as any opponent Sting had ever faced.

Warily Sting circled the robot, waiting for a chance to test its strength. He didn't have to wait long. The mechanical mangler moved in quickly and scooped Sting up in its steel sinewed arms. The robot slammed

Sting to the canvas. Now Sting knew how strong the robot was. Stronger than *anyone* he had ever fought before.

Rising to his feet, and shaking his head clear, Sting knew he would have to fight harder than ever before to defeat the Dangerous Alliance's latest weapon. Sting kept out of the mechanoid's reach, raining blow after blow onto its steel skull, but the metal menace just kept coming. lunging for Sting, the robot missed and stumbled into the ropes. As it bounced back Sting delivered a drop kick that would have floored any other wrestler. The robot rocked back, off balance for a second, before continuing its attack.

"Get him!" screamed Paul E. Dangerously at the ringside. "**Smash Sting!**"

With inhuman speed the robot landed a vicious forearm smash on Sting's chin, sending him reeling. Catching one of Sting's arms, the metal mauler executed an Irish Whip sending Sting careening into the corner post. Sting staggered into the centre of the ring, dazed by the speed and force of the robot's moves. Looking up he saw the metal monster bearing down on him, preparing to deliver a clothesline blow. At the last possible instant, Sting ducked the lethal stroke and with a mighty heave of his shoulders sent the robot up into the air and over onto its back.

The robot was fast and strong, but the robot was also heavy. Once down on the canvas it couldn't lift itself back onto its feet as quickly as a human wrestler.

Now Sting saw his chance. Grabbing the mechanoid's legs, he flipped it over onto its chest. The rest was second nature for Sting; it was time for his famous **Scorpion Deathlock**. The mechanical legs were locked in Sting's vice-like grip and he steadily began to apply pressure. No one and no thing had ever broken free from the

Scorpion Deathlock. With every ounce of strength, courage and determination in his body Sting kept the mechanical monster helpless. He knew that if he relaxed for a second the robot could break free, and it would only be a matter of time before it finished him.

The mechanoid however had not been programmed for courage and determination. Its computerised brain ran through a million calculations in a fraction of a second, but none could break the Scorpion Deathlock. Faced with such a fact the robot did the only logical thing to do...It **submitted**!

Paul E. Dangerously was **furious**! He had been so sure that his robot would defeat Sting. He had invested hundreds of thousands of dollars from the Dangerous Alliance in its construction and it had failed.

Sting strode triumphantly over to the ropes and looked down at Paul E. Dangerously. The sweat glistened on his aching muscles as he spoke to the humiliated executive.

"Mr Dangerously, you forgot **one** thing," he shouted above the roar of the crowd. "Your robot may have been programmed with every wrestling move in the rule book, but you can't programme a robot with courage and determination. Those are qualities only **humans** possess."

As Paul E. Dangerously and his defeated robot left the auditorium, Sting held his weary arms aloft and bathed in the frantic applause of the crowd. Never before had WCW witnessed such a wrestling match!

A ringside commentary by **Bambos**.

WCW

EL GIGANTE

The world's largest and tallest athlete was born in a very small village in Argentina. At school his size attracted attention and soon he was playing basketball, in which he dominated everybody. He was coached by the best and soon made the National Team. After achieving fame in South America, he was drafted by the Atlanta Hawks in Georgia. He didn't make the team but his popularity and his size alerted Ted Turner, owner of the Hawks and WCW. Since then **El Gigante** has been in training and though he is very new to pro wrestling, his size advantage more than makes up for it. His native language is Spanish, of course, but he is picking up English very quickly.

Height: 7'7"
Weight: 435 lbs
Chest: 72"
Waist: 48"
Shoe Size: 21

Favourite Food: Any kind and plenty of it
Favourite Music: Most kinds. Beatles and Janet Jackson.
Favourite Wrestler: Sting
Favourite Pastime: Shooting baskets, watching wrestling videos.

WCW SUPERSTAR SUPER MOVES

THE CLAWHOLD - Many professional wrestlers have attempted the Clawhold but never as effectively as El Gigante. The traditional clawhold is applied by placing the hand on the opponents head and then squeezing the head with the fingertips. If applied correctly the opponent will be brought to a standstill. El Gigante has a fantastic advantage over the other wrestlers - his hands are huge!

WCW

JOHNNY B. BADD

Take Little Richard's face, Charles Atlas' body and Marilyn Monroe's feather boa, put them all together and you get **Johnny B. Badd**, one of the most outrageous characters ever to hit WCW. But if any of his opponents think that all he can do is prance and dance around, they better think again. Managed by the always crafty Teddy Long, Johnny B. Badd looks likely to strut and preen his way to the top.

Height: 6'
Weight: 245 lbs

Hometown: Macon, Georgia
Favourite Holds: Left Hook - "the Tutti Fruiti"
Toughest Opponent: P.N. News
Greatest Achievement: Finding matching gold lame trunks and matching boa
Motto: "I'm so pretty I should have been born a little girl. But I'm a baaaaad man!"

WCW

P.N. NEWS

One of the most popular and enigmatic wrestlers to enter WCW in a long time, P.N.News is a huge rapmaster hailing from Motown. From the opening bass riff that marks his entrance, to the final crunch of the mat, shuddering beneath his devastating splash from the top rope, P.N. News delivers a crowd pleasing beat that rocks the joint.

Height: 6'2"
Weight: 404 lbs

Hometown: Motown
Favourite Hold: Splash - The Broken Record
Toughest Opponent: Hammer (on the charts) and Johnny B. Badd (in the ring)
Greatest Achievement: Watching his rap single go up and his opponents go down
Motto: "Yo baby, yo baby, yo baby, YO!"

HELLO AGAIN, WRESTLING FANS! *MISSY HYATT* HERE WITH ALL THE LATEST WRESTLING NEWS! AS Y'ALL KNOW, W.C.W. WORLD CHAMPION *LEX LUGER* WAFFLED *RON SIMMONS*, THE WINNER OF LAST WEEK'S OVER THE TOP ROPE BATTLE ROYAL, WITH THE PRESTIGIOUS WRESTLER OF THE YEAR TROPHY.

AS WINNER, SIMMONS WAS GRANTED A *SHOT* AT LUGER'S WORLD TITLE.

LUGER HAS MADE IT CLEAR ON MANY OCCASIONS THAT HE WILL *CRIPPLE* ANY AND ALL SERIOUS CHALLENGERS TO HIS CHAMPIONSHIP. SIMMONS HAS JUST SHOT TO THE HEAD OF LUGER'S *HIT LIST*.

AS A RESULT OF THIS *DEPLORABLE* ACT, THE W.C.W. CHAMPIONSHIP COMMITTEE IS RIGHT NOW DECIDING THE *FUTURE* OF "THE TOTAL PACKAGE" LEX LUGER'S WORLD HEAVYWEIGHT WRESTLING CHAMPIONSHIP.

LUGER *CONTINUES* TO BOAST HIS OWN BRAND OF RHETORIC.

SIMMONS HAS SUFFERED A HERNIATED DISC AS A RESULT OF LUGER'S *ATTITUDE ADJUSTMENT*--REPEATED *PILE DRIVERS* ON THE BROKEN TROPHY. SIMMONS' WRESTLING FUTURE IS NOW UNCERTAIN.

THIS JUST IN! THE W.C.W. CHAMPIONSHIP COMMITTEE HAS *JUST* DECIDED THAT LEX LUGER MUST *DEFEND* HIS TITLE AGAIN AT TONIGHT'S CLASH OF CHAMPIONS IN ATLANTA. BUT THAT'S NOT ALL--

LUGER MUST FACE THE TOP *THREE* CHALLENGERS IN A 3-ON-1 *HANDICAP MATCH!*

THIS IS *OUTRAGEOUS!* IT'S COMPLETELY *UNPRECEDENTED!* NEVER BEFORE HAS A CHAMPION HAD TO DEFEND HIS TITLE THIS WAY! DO YOU W.C.W. *PAPER PUSHERS* THINK YOU CAN WALK ALL OVER LEX LUGER?!

WELL, LET ME TELL YOU-- IT DOESN'T MATTER IF I FACE THREE MEN--OR *THIRTY!* I'M THE *TOTAL PACKAGE!* AND I CAN PUT TOGETHER *ANY* WINNING COMBINATION!

AND RON SIMMONS--THIS ISN'T OVER *YET.* DO YOURSELF A FAVOR. GET A JOB FLIPPING BURGERS SOMEWHERE. BECAUSE LEX LUGER *ALWAYS* HAS AN ANGLE!

THE CHAMPION IS CERTAINLY *IRATE*... AND AS YOU CAN HEAR--

CRASH!

THUD!

--LEX'S FURNITURE IS TAKING THE *BRUNT* OF HIS ANGER.

CRITICS ARGUE THAT LUGER HAS HELD W.C.W. UNDER HIS DARK CLOUD FOR TOO LONG...THAT TONIGHT'S MATCH-UP SHOULD SEE A NEW WORLD'S CHAMPION. BUT *WHO* WILL BE CHOSEN TO WRESTLE LEX? IF IT'S *DIAMOND STUDD, BIG VAN VADER* OR *JOHNNY B. BADD,* WE COULD BE GOING FROM OUT OF THE FRYING PAN AND INTO THE FIRE!

HEEL

AN EPIC TALE OF LYING & CHEATING BY:

"MAD DOG" MIKE LACKEY — WORDS
"RAMPAGING" RON WILSON — PICTURES
"DASTARDLY" DON HUDSON — INKS
"POWERFUL" PAUL BECTON — COLOURS
"COWARDLY" CLEM ROBINS — LETTERS
"MALICIOUS" MIKE ROCKWITZ — EDITS
"TREMENDOUS" TOM DeFALCO — REFEREE-IN-CHIEF

JIM ROSS HERE, FANS! SITTING IN FOR PAUL E. DANGEROUSLY IS TERRENCE TAYLOR!

THE COMPUTERIZED ANNOUNCER OF THE '90's!

BIG BARNEY and FERAL FRED AREN'T HAVING MUCH LUCK AGAINST THE STEINERS!

I'M SURPRISED AT THE STEINERS, MANHANDLING THE FODDER THAT WAY!

WELL, TERRENCE, YOU'VE BEEN KNOWN TO MANHANDLE YOUR OPPONENTS!

BUT NEVER MORE THAN WHAT MY COMPUTER SAID THEY COULD HANDLE!

LISTEN, I DON'T WANNA TALK ABOUT THE STEINERS! LET'S GO TO THE VIDEO TAPE!

SURPRISE, LEX! I'M ONE OF YOUR THREE OPPONENTS TONIGHT! THINK YOU CAN HANDLE BEING STINGERSIZED?

WHAT HAPPENED TO YOU, LEX? WE USED TO BE FRIENDS! THEN, YOU WON THE CHAMPIONSHIP, AND ALL THAT CHANGED!

NOW YOU THINK YOU CAN BULLDOZE OVER ANYONE WHO GETS IN YOUR WAY? WRONG! YER GOIN' DOWN, PAL!

STING IS THE FIRST MAN SELECTED FOR THIS *CONTROVERSIAL* CONTEST!

IT'S NOT *FAIR*, JIM ROSS! LEX SHOULD--*WOW!* A NASTY *SPIKE-PILE DRIVER!*

STICK A FORK IN HIM--HE'S *DONE!*

YOU DON'T NEED A *COMPUTER* TO SEE THAT THAT MOVE WAS *UNNECESSARY!*

WELL, IT'S TRUE THE STEINERS' *NEXT* CHALLENGE WILL BE MORE DIFFICULT!

STEINER BROTHERS! I'M *BOBBY EATON* AND I HATE YOUR GUTS! TELL 'EM, *ARN!*

YOU DRESS REAL FLASHY, STEINERS--THE CHICKS LOVE YA! AND *DOUBLE-A* WILL MAKE SURE THEY VISIT YOU--IN THE *HOSPITAL!*

IF ANYONE CAN TAKE DOWN THE STEINERS--IT'S *THESE GUYS!*

PLEASE, TERRENCE --LET'S GO TO MISSY FOR AN INTERVIEW!

WE LOVE YOU, WCW FANS! THIS IS THE *GREATEST* SPORT IN THE WORLD!

BUT EATON AND ANDERSON--YOU'RE THE BIGGEST *CHUMPS* IN THE WORLD!

YEAH! YOU'LL NEVER GET THE JUMP ON *US!*

WH-UNNNK

"HOW ABOUT A SNACK, YA LOSER?"

"BUNCH 'A COWARDS!"

"I'VE HAD ENOUGH!"

YAAAUGH!

"UNBELIEVABLE! THE STEINERS HAVE *DECIMATED* THEIR ATTACKERS!"

"ANDERSON AND EATON WILL BE *SELLING* HOT DOGS AFTER THIS FIASCO!"

"DON'T QUIT YOUR DAY JOBS! HA HA HA!"

"WELL SAID, SCOTT! SO, TERRENCE, CAN WE ASSUME *RON SIMMONS* WILL BE PART OF TONIGHT'S CONTEST?"

"AND WHAT ABOUT THE *Z-MAN?* EITHER OF THOSE TWO MEN COULD WIN IT ALL!"

"MY COMPUTER DOESN'T AGREE, ROSS! AND GUESS WHAT? *I* HAVE TAPE OF THE NEW *WCW MYSTERY MAN!*"

WHO?

"GREETINGS, FELLOW GRAPPLERS! I SINCERELY HOPE YOUR *INSURANCE* IS PAID UP, BECAUSE THE *GHOUL* IS IN TOWN. AND *YOU*, STING, ARE IN FOR A VERY *RUDE AWAKENING!*"

WCW

I DON'T THINK THE STINGER *WOULD* DO SOMETHING THAT *DESPICABLE!*

WELL, LUGER'S WRESTLING *SMART!* HE KNOWS HE HAS *THREE* MEN TO BEAT, AND IF HE CAN TAKE OUT Z-MAN WITH A *MINIMUM* OF EFFORT, THEN MORE POWER TO HIM.

WAKE UP, Z-MAN! *GET HIM!*

HERE COMES LUGER'S PATENTED *PILE DRIVER!*

IF HE SLAPS *THIS* ONE ON YOU, IT'S ALL OVER.

WAITAMINUTE! LUGER'S GOING TO PILEDRIVE Z-MAN ON TO THE BELT! HE'LL *BREAK* HIS NECK!

LEX LUGER IS JUST KEEPING HIS WORD. HE SAID HE WAS GONNA CRIPPLE *ANY* OPPOSITION, AND THAT'S WHAT HE'S DOING!

BESIDES, HE'S WRESTLING THREE TOP ATHLETES! HE CAN'T AFFORD TO BE ALL HUGS AND KISSES IN THERE!

WU — **NK!**

THAT'S JUST TERRIBLE... A *CHAMPION* SHOULDN'T CONDUCT HIMSELF LIKE *THAT!*

HE *WON,* DIDN'T HE?

BUT HE WON IN SUCH AN *UNDERHANDED* WAY! Z-MAN APPEARS TO BE OKAY. LET'S GO TO THE VIDEO--

Z-MAN? MORE LIKE *ZERO-MAN* AFTER THAT LAST FIGHT, BABY. DON'T WORRY, THOUGH-- I HEAR *BURGER WHIZ* IS HIRIN'! TEE-HEE!

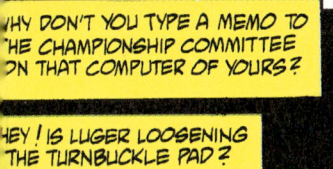

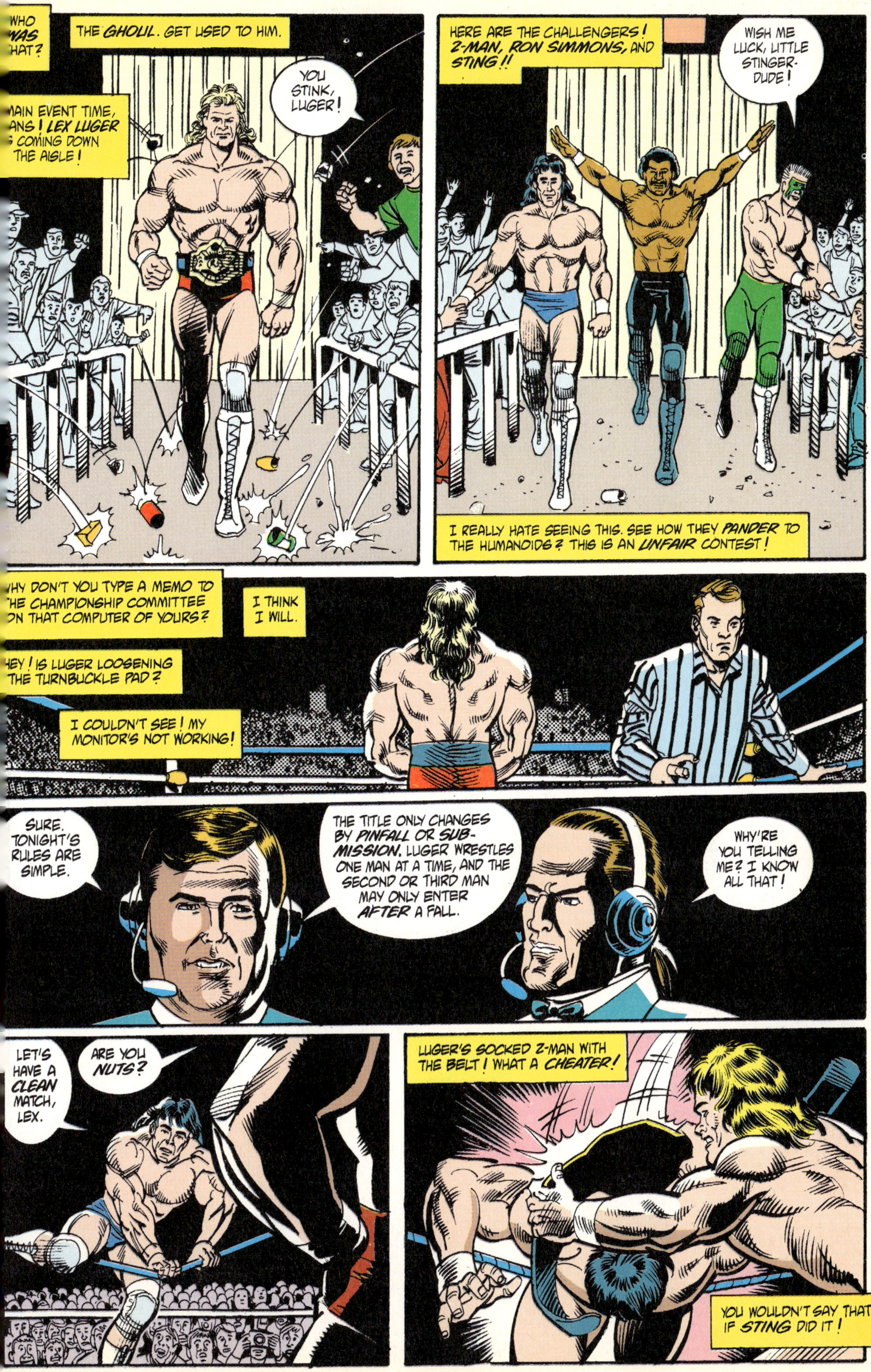

Panel 1:
WHO WAS THAT?
THE GHOUL. GET USED TO HIM.
MAIN EVENT TIME, FANS! LEX LUGER IS COMING DOWN THE AISLE!
YOU STINK, LUGER!

Panel 2:
HERE ARE THE CHALLENGERS! Z-MAN, RON SIMMONS, AND STING!!
WISH ME LUCK, LITTLE STINGER-DUDE!
I REALLY HATE SEEING THIS. SEE HOW THEY PANDER TO THE HUMANOIDS? THIS IS AN UNFAIR CONTEST!

Panel 3:
WHY DON'T YOU TYPE A MEMO TO THE CHAMPIONSHIP COMMITTEE ON THAT COMPUTER OF YOURS?
I THINK I WILL.
HEY! IS LUGER LOOSENING THE TURNBUCKLE PAD?
I COULDN'T SEE! MY MONITOR'S NOT WORKING!

Panel 4:
SURE. TONIGHT'S RULES ARE SIMPLE.
THE TITLE ONLY CHANGES BY PINFALL OR SUBMISSION. LUGER WRESTLES ONE MAN AT A TIME, AND THE SECOND OR THIRD MAN MAY ONLY ENTER AFTER A FALL.
WHY'RE YOU TELLING ME? I KNOW ALL THAT!

Panel 5:
LET'S HAVE A CLEAN MATCH, LEX.
ARE YOU NUTS?

Panel 6:
LUGER'S SOCKED Z-MAN WITH THE BELT! WHAT A CHEATER!
YOU WOULDN'T SAY THAT IF STING DID IT!

OH GOODY. NOTHING I LIKE *BETTER* THAN WATCHING STING GET BEATEN UP!

WE'LL *SEE* ABOUT THAT! STING'S HAVING WORDS WITH LUGER--

YOU LOUSY CRUMB, LEX! WHY'D YOU *DO* IT? WHAT WENT WRONG?

AH, SHUT UP, YOU *CRYBABY.*

YOU ASKED FOR IT--!

I'M NOT GONNA WATCH YOU *ABUSE* THAT TITLE ANY MORE!

UGHF!

STING'S THE *REAL* THING!

WHERE ARE YOUR SNIDE COMMENTS *NOW*, TERRENCE?

HE WON'T BE ABLE TO DO THAT TO *THE GHOUL!*

—AND THE CHAMP IS HIGH-TAILING IT OUT OF THE RING!

NO--HE'S JUST RESTING! A TRUE CHAMPION!

HI, LEX. REMEMBER ME?

HEY--IT'S COOL, MAN! SORRY ABOUT THAT TROPHY!

YEAH, SURE!

FORGET ABOUT THE TROPHY. IT'S YOUR BELT I WANT *NOW*.

SIMMONS *CAN'T* HIT HIM YET! THAT'S ILLEGAL!

HE WANTS LEX IN THE RING--

--AND I FOR ONE DON'T *BLAME* HIM.

YO, STING!

SHUT UP! WHEN DID *YOU* EVER WRESTLE?

GRACIAS, DUDE!

WAIT-- GIMME A MINIT--

IRISH WHIP INTO THE CORNER--

UOOGHF!

READY, LEX?

TIME TO GET STINGERSIZED!

I CAN'T LOOK!

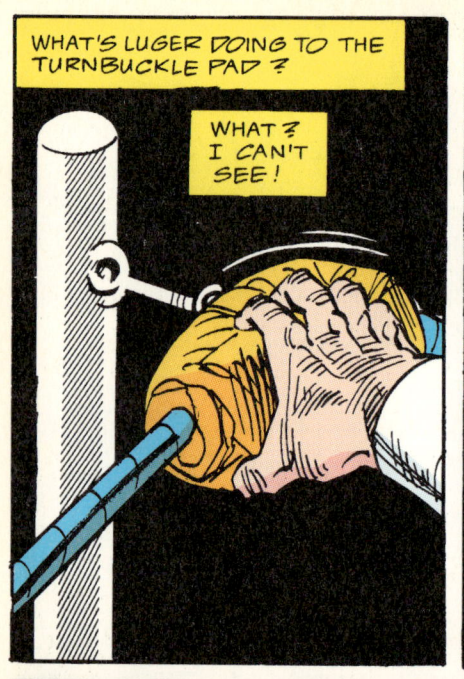

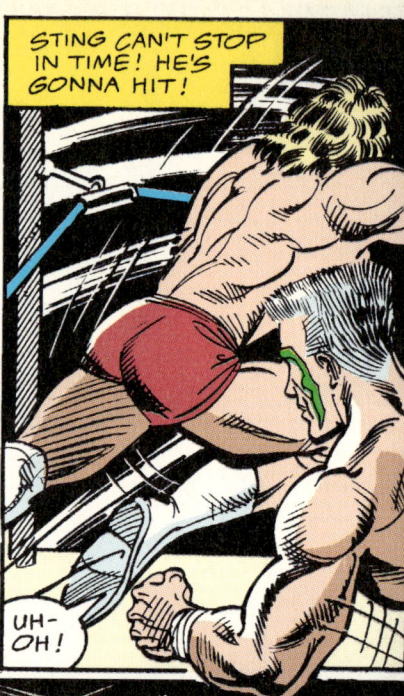

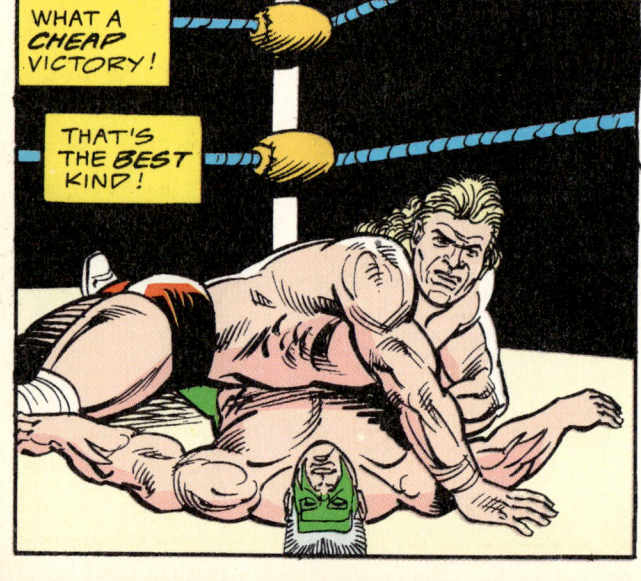

Panel	Text

Panel 1: WHAT'S LUGER DOING TO THE TURNBUCKLE PAD?
WHAT? I CAN'T SEE!

Panel 2: HE'S TORN IT RIGHT OFF! HE'S EXPOSED THE *STEEL* TURNBUCKLE!

Panel 3: STING CAN'T STOP IN TIME! HE'S GONNA HIT!
UH-OH!

Panel 4: THUDD!
WHAT A DISGRACE!
I DIDN'T SEE--MY MONITOR BLANKED OUT AGAIN!

Panel 5: WHAT A *CHEAP* VICTORY!
THAT'S THE *BEST* KIND!

Panel 6: LEX LUGER--I'M COMING AFTER YOU AND YOUR TITLE. YOU *CAN'T* CRIPPLE ME!

HEY-- HIS HEAD *DENTED* THE RING POST!

TERRENCE, *PLEASE!*

STING? ANY WORDS FOR THE FANS? STING? HELLO?

I *HOPE* HE'S ALL RIGHT!

ACTUALLY, JIM, THAT'S WHAT STING WILL LOOK LIKE AFTER HE MEETS THE GHOUL.

ENOUGH, ALREADY! WHO *IS* THE GHOUL?

NOT TELLING.

ADMIT IT, TERRENCE. YOU DON'T EVEN KNOW!

OH, YES I DO!

WHACK!

HE'S *NOT* RON SIMMONS.

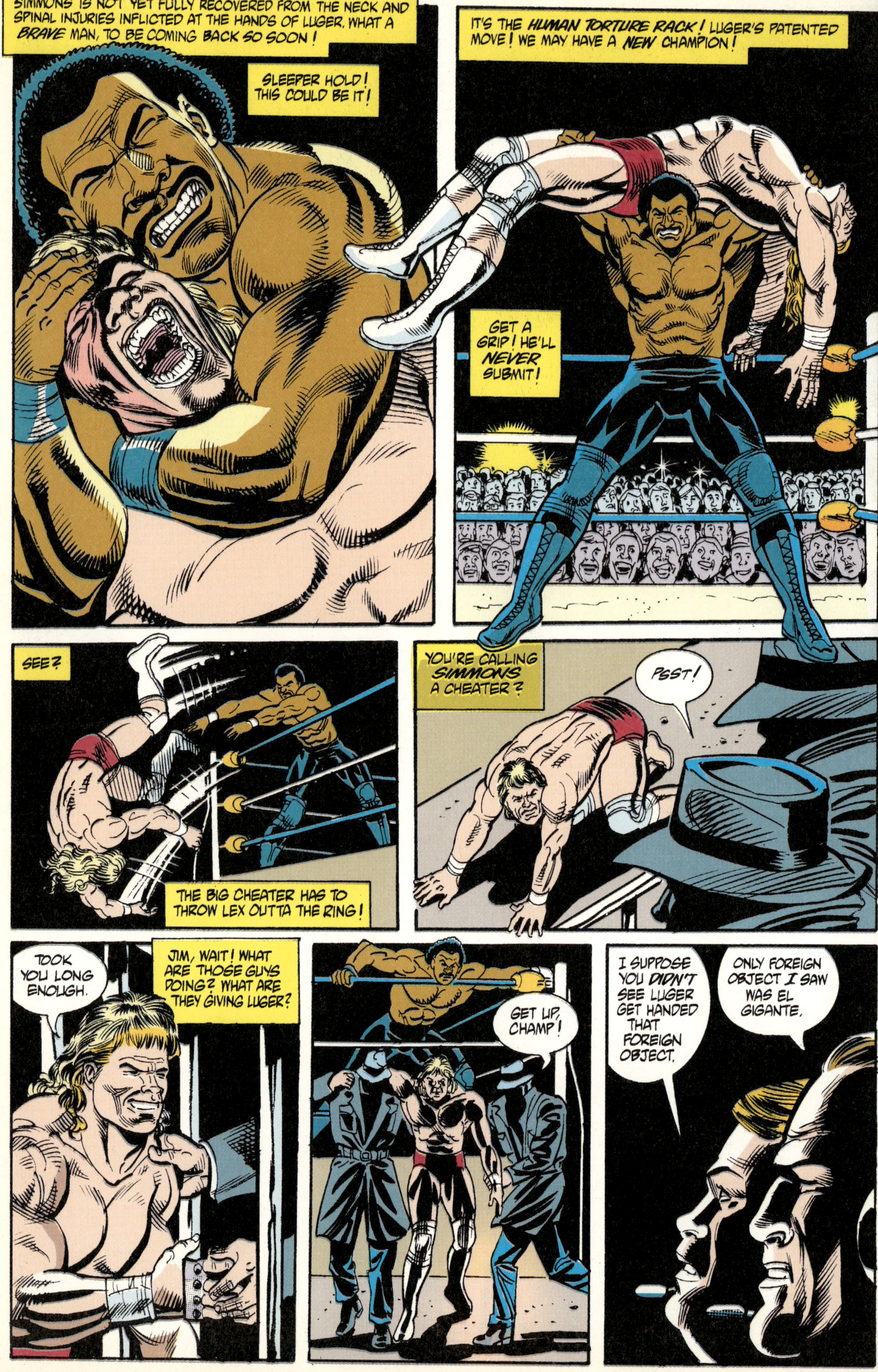
SIMMONS IS NOT YET FULLY RECOVERED FROM THE NECK AND SPINAL INJURIES INFLICTED AT THE HANDS OF LUGER. WHAT A *BRAVE* MAN, TO BE COMING BACK SO SOON!
SLEEPER HOLD! THIS COULD BE IT!
IT'S THE *HUMAN TORTURE RACK*! LUGER'S PATENTED MOVE! WE MAY HAVE A *NEW* CHAMPION!
GET A GRIP! HE'LL *NEVER* SUBMIT!
SEE?
THE BIG CHEATER HAS TO THROW LEX OUTTA THE RING!
YOU'RE CALLING *SIMMONS* A CHEATER?
PSST!
TOOK YOU LONG ENOUGH.
JIM, WAIT! WHAT ARE THOSE GUYS DOING? WHAT ARE THEY GIVING LUGER?
GET UP, CHAMP!
I SUPPOSE YOU *DIDN'T* SEE LUGER GET HANDED THAT FOREIGN OBJECT.
ONLY FOREIGN OBJECT *I* SAW WAS EL GIGANTE.

HOLD IT, CHUMP--

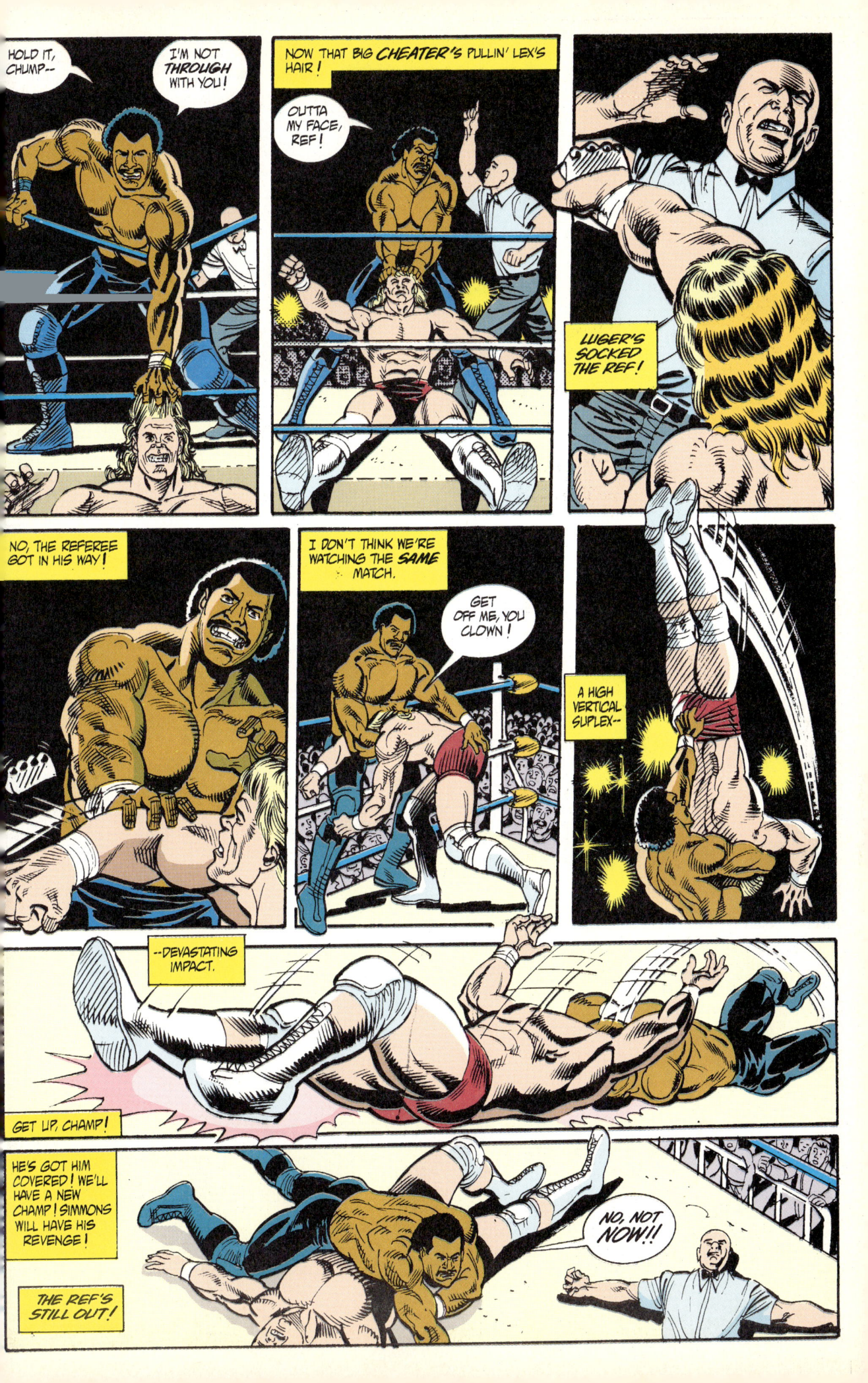

I'M NOT *THROUGH* WITH YOU!

NOW THAT BIG *CHEATER'S* PULLIN' LEX'S HAIR!

OUTTA MY FACE, REF!

LUGER'S SOCKED THE REF!

NO, THE REFEREE GOT IN HIS WAY!

I DON'T THINK WE'RE WATCHING THE *SAME* MATCH.

GET OFF ME, YOU CLOWN!

A HIGH VERTICAL SUPLEX--

--DEVASTATING IMPACT.

GET UP, CHAMP!

HE'S GOT HIM COVERED! WE'LL HAVE A NEW CHAMP! SIMMONS WILL HAVE HIS REVENGE!

THE REF'S STILL OUT!

NO, NOT *NOW*!!

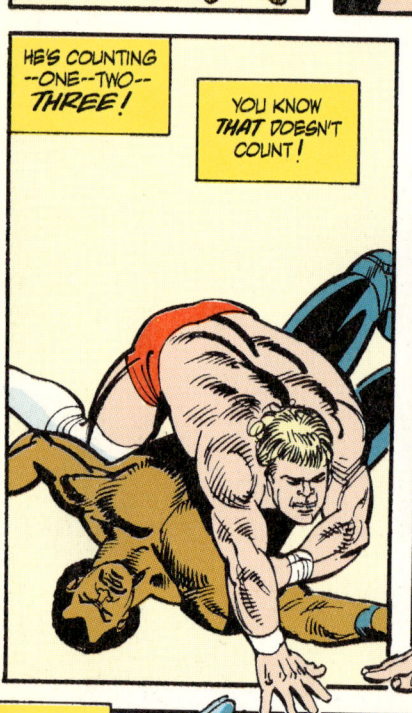

Panel 1: ONE--TWO--THREE!

Panel 2: MEANS NOTHIN'!

Panel 3: GET UP, REF! I'VE GOT HIM BEAT!

Panel 4: DON'T TURN YOUR BACK ON LUGER--

Panel 5: TURN AROUND, RON!

Panel 6: FORGET ABOUT HIM, SIMMONS!

Panel 7: UGH!

Panel 8: HE'S COUNTING --ONE--TWO-- THREE! YOU KNOW THAT DOESN'T COUNT!

Panel 9: WHY'S LEX YELLING AT THE REF? HE KNOCKED HIM OUT! YOU *@$!*ING STUPID--!

Panel 10: HE COULD'VE PUT SIMMONS AWAY, THAT'S WHY! SIMMONS HAD BETTER PAY ATTENTION!

Panel 11: OH NO, A PILE DRIVER! DO IT AGAIN! I LOVE THAT MOVE!

Panel 12: I THOUGHT PAUL E. DANGEROUSLY WAS TWISTED--! 1-2--

Panel 13: SIMMONS KICKED OUT! HE HAS GOT TO BE HURTING! WHAT AN ATHLETE!

"U MEAN E AGREE ON OMETHING?"

"NO, I WAS TALKING ABOUT *LUGER*!"

EVERYTHING'S GOING THE CHAMPION'S WAY...

"ONE-- TWO--"

"WHAT INTESTINAL FORTITUDE! HIS WHOLE BODY MUST BE IN AGONY!"

"SHUT UP, REF!"

"NO!!"

"LUGER BETTER WATCH OUT!"

"SIMMONS HAS ROLLED UP LUGER!"

"ONE--"

"TWO--"

"WAIT! LUGER'S GOT HIM!"

1-2-3!

"HEY, WAIT A SECOND! ONE OF LUGER'S MEN IS INTERFERING!"

LUGER'S WON AGAIN!!

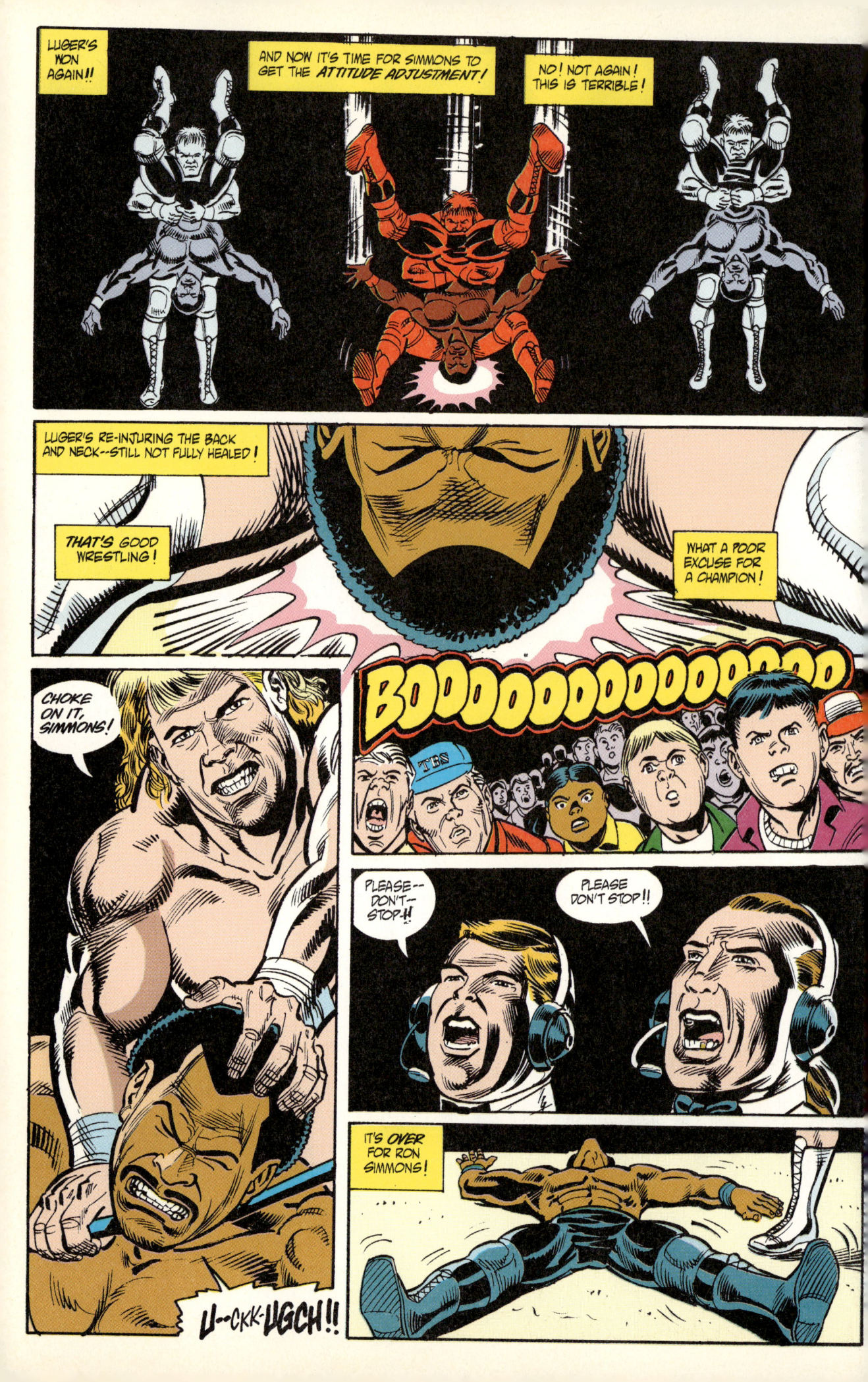

AND NOW IT'S TIME FOR SIMMONS TO GET THE *ATTITUDE ADJUSTMENT!*

NO! NOT AGAIN! THIS IS TERRIBLE!

LUGER'S RE-INJURING THE BACK AND NECK--STILL NOT FULLY HEALED!

THAT'S GOOD WRESTLING!

WHAT A POOR EXCUSE FOR A CHAMPION!

BOOOOOOOOOOOOOO

CHOKE ON IT, SIMMONS!

PLEASE-- DON'T-- STOP--!!

PLEASE DON'T STOP!!

IT'S *OVER* FOR RON SIMMONS!

U--CKK--UGCH!!

THE WINNER-- AND **STILL** WCW WORLD HEAVYWEIGHT WRESTLING CHAMPION-- LEX LUUUUUUGERRRR!!

I DON'T BELIEVE THIS! IT'S A TRAVESTY!

I KNOW--HE SHOULD PILE DRIVE SIMMONS *AGAIN*!

YOU CAN BET THE CHAMPIONSHIP COMMITTEE WILL HAVE SOMETHING TO SAY ABOUT THIS!

YEAH, "CONGRATULATIONS, CHAMP!"

BOO BOO BOO

I DON'T THINK SO.

HERE COMES TROUBLE!

EL GIGANTE'S GOT *NO* BUSINESS HERE!

I'M COMING FOR *YOU*, LUGER!

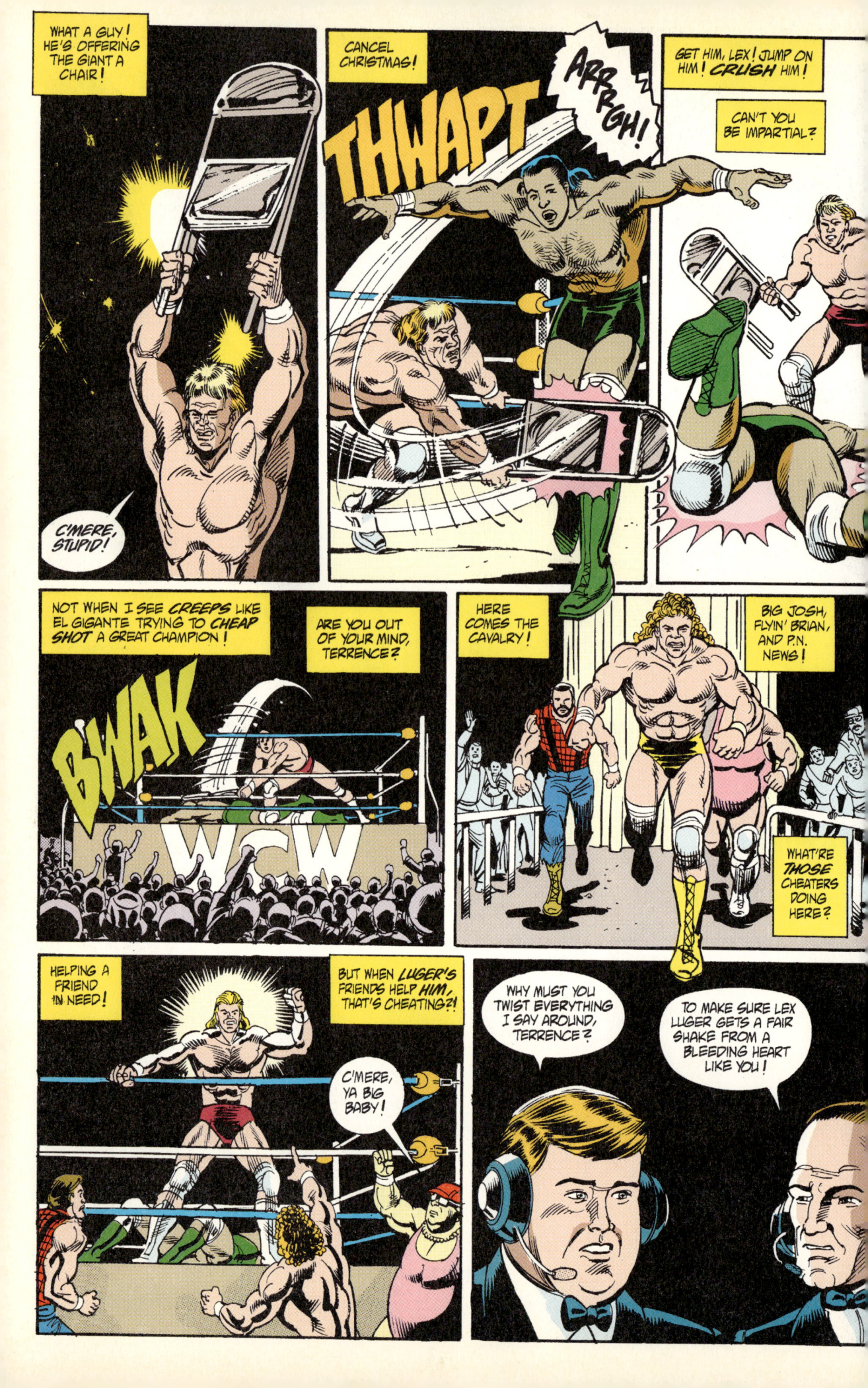

Panel	Text
1	WHAT A GUY! HE'S OFFERING THE GIANT A CHAIR! / C'MERE, STUPID!
2	CANCEL CHRISTMAS! / THWAPT / ARRRGH!
3	GET HIM, LEX! JUMP ON HIM! CRUSH HIM! / CAN'T YOU BE IMPARTIAL?
4	NOT WHEN I SEE CREEPS LIKE EL GIGANTE TRYING TO CHEAP SHOT A GREAT CHAMPION! / ARE YOU OUT OF YOUR MIND, TERRENCE? / BWAK
5	HERE COMES THE CAVALRY! / BIG JOSH, FLYIN' BRIAN, AND P.N. NEWS! / WHAT'RE THOSE CHEATERS DOING HERE?
6	HELPING A FRIEND IN NEED! / BUT WHEN LUGER'S FRIENDS HELP HIM, THAT'S CHEATING?! / C'MERE, YA BIG BABY!
7	WHY MUST YOU TWIST EVERYTHING I SAY AROUND, TERRENCE? / TO MAKE SURE LEX LUGER GETS A FAIR SHAKE FROM A BLEEDING HEART LIKE YOU!

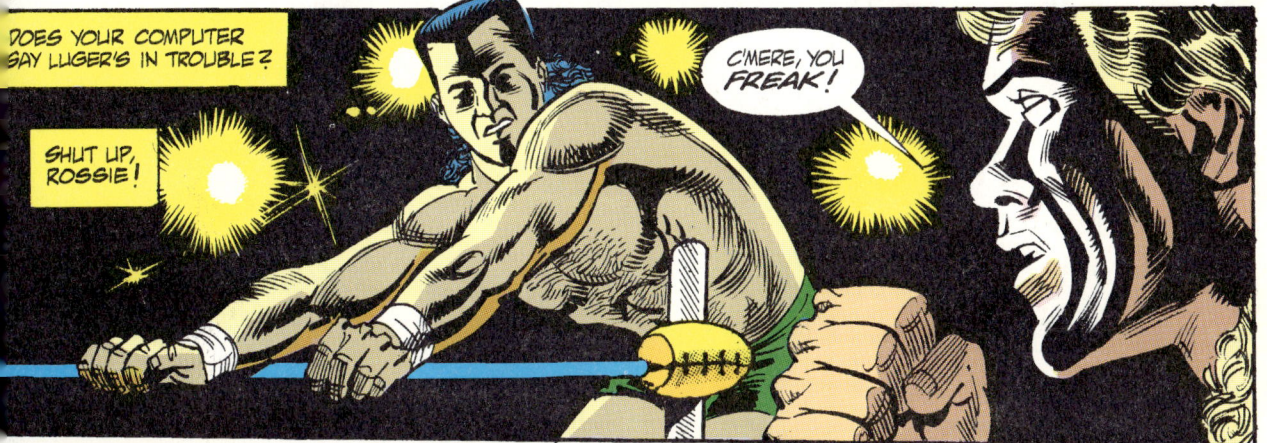

THE GIANT'S ON HIS FEET!

RUN, LEX! GET OUT OF THERE! OH NO!

NOW I'M MAD, LUGER!

I'M GONNA BREAK YOU IN HALF!

JOFGH!

AND YOUR STOOGES CAN'T HELP YOU!

GAAAAH!

DOES YOUR COMPUTER SAY LUGER'S IN TROUBLE?

SHUT UP, ROSSIE!

C'MERE, YOU FREAK!

BONK

YES! HIT 'M AGAIN!

THWAP!

YEAH! RIGHT IN THE BEAN!

THE GIANT'S DOWN!

AND WHAT A DENT HE MADE IN THE BELT!

LET'S GO TO MISSY FOR AN INTERVIEW--

I SAID I'D DO IT --AND I DID IT!

I CRUSHED THE BEST YOU HAD! NOW YOUR Z-MANS--AND YOUR STINGERS-- AND YOUR GIANTS-- ALL FINISHED!

BUT NOW WHAT'S LEFT? I'VE BEATEN THEM ALL! AND WHEN YOU'VE BEATEN THE BEST--YOU ARE THE BEST! AND I--AM--THE BEST!!

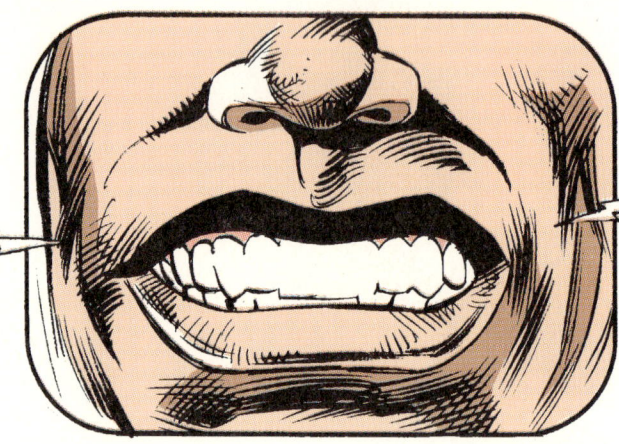

EL GIGANTE --FREE ADVICE. QUIT WRESTLING AND GET A JOB CHANGING STREET LIGHTS. BECAUSE YOU DON'T HAVE WHAT IT TAKES TO GET BY IN THIS SPORT.

AND NOW, DEAR MISSY, WITH A TEAR IN MY EYE, I TAKE MY LEAVE. GREENER PASTURES AWAIT THE TOTAL PACKAGE.

DON'T WORRY WHERE I AM--OR HOW I'LL GET BY, BECAUSE LEX LUGER ALWAYS HAS AN ANGLE!

THE END.